Deepening the Mystery

A Guided Journal Through Mystagogia

Deepening the Mystery

A Guided Journal Through Mystagogia

BLESSIE LA SCOLA

Copyright © 2023 by Blessie La Scola

All rights reserved. No part of this publication may be reproduced, distributed, or transmitted in any form or by any means, including photocopying, recording, or other electronic or mechanical methods, without the prior written permission of the copyright owner and the publisher, except in the case of brief quotations embodied in critical reviews and certain other noncommercial uses permitted by copyright law. For permission requests, write to the publisher, addressed "Attention: Permissions Coordinator," at the address below.

ARPress
45 Dan Road Suite 5
Canton, MA 02021

Hotline: 1(888) 821-0229
Fax: 1(508) 545-7580

Ordering Information:

Quantity sales. Special discounts are available on quantity purchases by corporations, associations, and others. For details, contact the publisher at the address above.

Printed in the United States of America.

ISBN-13:	Softcover	979-8-89330-882-2
	eBook	979-8-89330-884-6
	Hardback	979-8-89330-883-9

Library of Congress Control Number: 2024902525

CONTENTS

INTRODUCTION v
OPTIONS FOR USING YOUR JOURNAL vii
Week One 1
Week Two 2
Week Three 3
Week Four 4
Week Five 5
Week Six 6
Week Seven 7
Week Eight 8
Week Nine 9
Week Ten 10
Week Eleven 11
Week Twelve 12
Week Thirteen 13
Week Fourteen 14
Week Fifteen 15
Week Sixteen 16
Week Seventeen 17
Week Eighteen 18
Week Nineteen 19
Week Twenty 20
Week Twenty-one 21
Week Twenty-two 22
Week Twenty-three 23
Week Twenty-four 24
Week Twenty-five 25
Week Twenty-six 26

Week Twenty-seven	27
Week Twenty-eight	28
Week Twenty-nine	29
Week Thirty	30
Week Thirty-one	31
Week Thirty-two	32
Week Thirty-three	33
Week Thirty-four	34
Week Thirty-five	35
Week Thirty-six	36
Week Thirty-seven	37
Week Thirty-eight	38
Week Thirty-nine	39
Week Forty	40
Week Forty-one	41
Week Forty-two	42
Week Forty-three	43
Week Forty-four	44
Week Forty-five	45
Week Forty-six	46
Week Forty-seven	47
Week Forty-eight	48
Week Forty-nine	49
Week Fifty	50
Week Fifty-one	51
Week Fifty-two	52

I dedicate this journal to all those who have journeyed through any spiritual and religious encounter with God. May each day be another discovery into the mystery of what God calls and entices us to.

To my husband, who continues to challenge me to celebrate God's mystery.

INTRODUCTION

Welcome and congratulations to you who have experienced the process of the Christian Initiation for adults, youth, and children. This is a resource for you to use during this next year. It is also for any of you who have received any of the sacraments of initiation and those involved with you, as parents, sponsors, team, etc.

The journal is provided to serve you through the final period of the initiation process called Mystagogia. This period is for one year (52 weeks) following initiation. Its purpose is for all initiated to reflect, pray, discern, and discover the depth of Christ's love for them and a way to respond in service to Christ and his church.

I hope this journal will offer some guidance in breaking open the mysteries as you continue to grow in faith.

OPTIONS FOR USING YOUR JOURNAL

Your journal is filled with statements and questions to be completed or pondered upon. There is a focus for each week on which to center your thoughts or writings. For each day of the week, you will find a question or statement and you are encouraged to either write or reflect on your thoughts.

If you find that "Day 1" needs more than a day of thought, please take the time; if you discover that one of the questions or statements requires your attention but it is a different day of the week, no problem; do what you need to do, this is your journal. You may realize that this journal takes longer than a year to go through, one week or one question may require more time. There may be a question or statement you feel unprepared to reflect on; highlight or mark it and return to it later when ready. You are in formation with God and not limited by time.

You will find that many of the themes relate back to those that you were introduced to through the initiation process. This is to help you to re-connect to all that took place in your faith journey and to go deeper in your conversion experience.

Week One
Focus: *Easter Initiation, New Life*

Day 1 After I completed initiation, I experienced…

Day 2 What words of New Life will, or did I offer today?

Day 3 Where do I find signs of New Life around me?

Day 4 How do I experience things differently as a result of my initiation?

Day 5 What difference does my New Life make today in my response to others (patience, compassion, etc.)?

Day 6 In what way will I bring New Life to others?

Day 7 In what way have I accepted New Life from others?

Week Two
Focus: *Where to go from here...*

Day 1   How will I allow God to nourish me?

Day 2   How open am I to God's plan for my life?

Day 3   How have I seen Gods plan for me take form?

Day 4   In what way do I appreciate the talents God has given me?

Day 5   In what way will I serve others today?

Day 6   When and how do I find time to listen to God?

Day 7   How do I recognize that God is leading me?

Week Three

Focus: *Looking Back…remembering….*

Day 1   What first interested me in the Catholic Church?

Day 2   How did I experience the call to join the process of initiation?

Day 3   What feelings did I have as I recognized a need to respond?

Day 4   What circumstances in my life caused me to respond?

Day 5   What hesitations did I have?

Day 6   What positive or negative feelings were in those around me?

Day 7   What most influenced me to join the process?

Week Four
Focus: *Belonging*

Day 1   How has my experience of belonging changed?

Day 2   What feelings of welcome do I have as a part of community?

Day 3   In what way have I welcomed others into community?

Day 4   Where do I welcome the stranger?

Day 5   How do I experience interconnectedness in my community?

Day 6   What image symbolizes communal relationship?

Day 7   What does belonging cost?

Week Five
Focus: *Trust*

Day 1   How has my experience of trust deepened?

Day 2   What challenges my ability to trust?

Day 3   How do I reaffirm my trust in the presence of doubt?

Day 4   How do I see myself as trustworthy?

Day 5   What do I use to cultivate a habit of trust?

Day 6   What do I do to increase my trustworthiness?

Day 7   What are some ways that I encourage others to trust?

Week Six
Focus: *Searching for God and Truth*

Day 1   Where was I in life's journey when I recognized my need for God?

Day 2   Did I pursue God or did God pursue me?

Day 3   How did I realize that I had found God?

Day 4   What actions am I taking to uncover a deeper presence of God?

Day 5   How has knowing God affected my relationships?

Day 6   How has my understanding of my need for God increased?

Day 7   Where have I introduced others to God?

Week Seven
Focus: *Faith*

Day 1   Having faith is like…

Day 2   My faith is strongest when…. Weakest when….

Day 3   I am most challenged by the teachings of my faith when….

Day 4   What is the role of prayer in my faith journey?

Day 5   How do I allow others to affect my faith life?

Day 6   In what way do I reveal my faith in God to the world?

Day 7   My faith is nourished most by…

Week Eight
Focus: *In the Image of God*

Day 1   The image of God I have today is....

Day 2   I see God's image most in....

Day 3   What steps did I take to help me see Gods image in others?

Day 4   What helps me see God's image in those persons who offer me challenge?

Day 5   How do I try to make God's image visible in myself or through my actions?

Day 6   How do I encourage those around me to see God in others?

Day 7   In what way do I challenge others to live out the image of God?

Week Nine
Focus: *The Bible*

Day 1   What makes reading and praying with Scripture important for my faith life?

Day 2   What are any obstacles that prevent me from taking more time for the Scriptures?

Day 3   What stories and events of the Bible do I remember as being most influential?

Day 4   Recently, how have I been challenged by a reading from the Bible?

Day 5   When do I share what I have heard from Scripture with others?

Day 6   How have I patterned my life according to the teachings from the Bible?

Day 7   What quote from the Bible do I know by heart? Why?

Week Ten
Focus: *Tour of the Church*

Day 1   As I enter Church what feelings come over me?

Day 2   What do I notice first as I take my place in church? Why?

Day 3   What meaning does the altar have for my life?

Day 4   The Crucifix calls me to....

Day 5   Which Station of the Cross do I most relate to? Why?

Day 6   How am I challenged to grow by the community I celebrate with?

Day 7   As I leave Church, I feel…

Week Eleven
Focus: *Tour of the Church*

Day 1   The Ambo, where the Word of God is proclaimed, is important to me because…

Day 2   How important to me are the Sacred Oils and why?

Day 3   What feelings come over me as I reflect upon the Baptismal Font?

Day 4   What specific religious piece in the church building draws me to prayer?

Day 5   The Paschal Candle reminds me of…

Day 6   The windows of the church building call me to…

Day 7   What do I remember about the church building that gives me comfort during the weekdays?

Week Twelve
Focus: *The Celebration of Mass*

Day 1   I look forward to going to Mass because…

Day 2   As Mass begins, I feel…

Day 3   In what way does The Word of God nourish me?

Day 4   How does the Gospel challenge me to grow?

Day 5   How am I called to conversion during the Eucharistic Prayer?

Day 6   What are my thoughts and feelings as I receive the Body and Blood of Christ?

Day 7   How am I challenged when I hear the words, "Go to love and serve the Lord"?

Week Thirteen
Focus: *The Celebration of Mass*

Day 1   During the Gathering Rite, the introduction, I experience…

Day 2   As I make the Sign of The Cross, I feel…

Day 3   The Responsorial Psalm gives me…

Day 4   What do I understand my role to be during the Prayers of the Faithful?

Day 5   What feelings come over me while saying the Lord's Prayer in community?

Day 6   What is my role during the Eucharistic Prayer?

Day 7   In what way does the Gathering Rite prepare me to receive Holy Communion?

Week Fourteen
Focus: *Our Identity in Christ*

Day 1   In what way am I most profoundly different since beginning the initiation process?

Day 2   In what way am I continually called to change?

Day 3   Where in my life am I most challenged to show my identity in Christ?

Day 4   When and where do I find myself most free to share my identity in Christ?

Day 5   How do I affirm my decision to be identified as a follower of Christ?

Day 6   In what way do I affirm others to live their identity in Christ?

Day 7   How does the Eucharist continue to call me to become all that Christ calls me to be?

Week Fifteen
Focus: *Revelation of God*

Day 1   How do I respond to God's Presence?

Day 2   In what way do I see my family/friends responding to God's presence?

Day 3   What challenges have I received from the presence of God in my life?

Day 4   How has the presence of God encouraged hope in my life?

Day 5   Where and how often do I find God's presence in the world?

Day 6   In which Scripture passages do I find God revealing God's self to me?

Day 7   Where and how often do I reveal the presence of God to others?

Week Sixteen
Focus: *Prayer in my life*

Day 1   Why do I talk to God in prayer?

Day 2   What have I gained in relationship with God through prayer?

Day 3   What do I need to encourage prayer in my life?

Day 4   What importance does silence play in my daily life?

Day 5   What am I doing to improve my skill in listening to God?

Day 6   Why do I pray the way I do?

Day 7   When have I taught another person to pray?

Week Seventeen
Focus: *Acceptance of the Cross*

Day 1   How has my understanding of acceptance of the cross in my life grown?

Day 2   In what way has accepting the cross given me strength?

Day 3   Where have I offered sacrifice through service to others?

Day 4   Where have I seen signs of the cross in the actions of others?

Day 5   How will/did I speak words of love today?

Day 6   Am I able to receive words of love?

Day 7   When others see me do they see a living sign of the cross?

Week Eighteen
Focus: *The Gospel As a Way of Life*

Day 1   In what way am I a sign of God's Love to others?

Day 2   How has my faith been strengthened by the gospel message?

Day 3   Where am I most challenged in living out the Gospel message?

Day 4   When in my life has the gospel been most welcomed?

Day 5   How does my prayer life reflect the gospel?

Day 6   What is my favorite gospel teaching and why?

Day 7   If I were to become one word of the gospel – what would that word be?

Week Nineteen
Focus: *Rite of Welcome/*
Rite of Acceptance into Order of Catechumen

Day 1   In what way have I become more welcoming and accepting of others?

Day 2   In what way have I allowed myself to be welcomed or accepted?

Day 3   What fears or challenges still hamper my acceptance or welcoming of others?

Day 4   What examples do I find in my faith community of being welcoming and accepting of others?

Day 5   In what way do I see myself taking part in my faith community's efforts to be welcoming and accepting?

Day 6   Am I willing to risk being an example of accepting others as Christ does?

Day 7   What step will I take to bring further acceptance of others into the world?

Week Twenty
Focus: *Dismissal Rite, Breaking open the Word*

Day 1   What effect does it have upon the community when catechumens are dismissed?

Day 2   When the catechumens are dismissed, I feel…

Day 3   When do I "break open" the Word of God during the week?

Day 4   What relationship is there to the "breaking open of the Word" and to the "Breaking of the Bread" during mass?

Day 5   What changes in my life can be attributed to reflecting upon God's Word?

Day 6   In what way has the Word given me courage to speak the truth to others?

Day 7   Where in my life do I have support or guidance in understanding God's Word for my life?

Week Twenty-one
Focus: *To be Anointed*

Day 1   As I was anointed with the Holy Oil, I felt…

Day 2   As the anointing took place, I felt called to…

Day 3   Being anointed with oil meant…

Day 4   What impression did the anointing I received make upon others who were present?

Day 5   In what way has the anointing of oil permeated my life?

Day 6   When did I last share my experience of being anointed?

Day 7   In what way has being "one of the anointed in Christ" changed my perception of myself and others?

Week Twenty-two
Focus: *The Creed, Our statement of belief*

Day 1   How have I made the Trinity visible in my life?

Day 2   I am drawn to God our creator when…

Day 3   My relationship with Jesus is…

Day 4   The Holy Spirit challenges me by…

Day 5   I live my baptismal call-in community by…

Day 6   How do I live out the words, "one, holy, catholic and apostolic"?

Day 7   The promise of eternal life calls me to change my actions by…

Week Twenty-three
Focus: *The Sacrament of Baptism*

Day 1   When I reflect on my baptism, I think of…

Day 2   Because of my baptism I have…

Day 3   The water of Baptism calls me to…

Day 4   In what way has the Light of Christ within me lit the way for others?

Day 5   In what way have I come to understand more deeply "dying to my old life"?

Day 6   How am I recognized as being "clothed in Christ"?

Day 7   The one symbol of baptism that touches me the most is…

Week Twenty-four
Focus: *The Sacrament of Confirmation*

Day 1   Through Confirmation Christ calls me to…

Day 2   What has changed in my life as a result of my confirmation?

Day 3   How has my being confirmed affected others around me?

Day 4   What gifts of the Holy Spirit continue to be stirred within me?

Day 5   In what way have I made the gifts of the Holy Spirit known?

Day 6   The seal of the Holy Spirit offers me…

Day 7   In what way has my faith been strengthened by the Holy Spirit?

Week Twenty-five
Focus: *The Sacrament of Holy Communion, Eucharist*

Day 1   The first time I received the Eucharist I felt...

Day 2   How has receiving the Eucharist deepened my understanding of Christ's presence in my life?

Day 3   In what way do I envision myself as part of the Body of Christ?

Day 4   How has being part of Christ's Body affected my actions outside of liturgy?

Day 5   When I sit in prayer with the Blessed Sacrament....

Day 6   Where do I offer Eucharist through my actions to others?

Day 7   In what ways has my hunger for Eucharist grown?

Week Twenty-six
Focus: *The Sacrament of Reconciliation*

Day 1   When I first celebrated this sacrament, I felt…

Day 2   When I celebrate this sacrament now, I feel…

Day 3   In what way have I become more aware of my need for this sacrament?

Day 4   Celebrating this sacrament causes me to….

Day 5   In what way has my understanding of sin changed?

Day 6   How has my awareness of grace affected my life?

Day 7   How am I a reconciling agent for the world?

Week Twenty-seven
Focus: *The Sacrament of Anointing of the Sick*

Day 1   When I witness the celebration of the sacrament of anointing of the sick, I feel…

Day 2   In what way do I need healing?

Day 3   In what way do community relationships encourage healing?

Day 4   How does the power of prayer offer healing in my life and that of others?

Day 5   Where in my life do I reveal the gift of compassion?

Day 6   How does the Body of Christ recognize and respond to its brokenness and need for healing?

Day 7   What will I do to help in healing the world?

Week Twenty-eight

Focus: *The Sacrament of Marriage, a Vocation*

Day 1   What is my understanding of the sacrament of marriage?

Day 2   How has the sacrament of marriage as a vocation affected me as an individual?

Day 3   How am I challenged when I hear that the church is the bride of Christ?

Day 4   In what way have I been called to a vocation in relationship with Christ?

Day 5   My church community has heard the call to their vocation in Christ by…

Day 6   In what way do I submit myself to Christ?

Day 7   How does my acceptance of my vocation affect my decisions and actions?

Twenty-nine

Focus: *The Sacrament of Holy Orders, Vocation of Priesthood*

Day 1   What do I appreciate about my parish priests?

Day 2   How does my participation in the priesthood of Christ challenge me?

Day 3   How do I experience the living word of God through the priests of the church?

Day 4   How have the priests I know given me guidance or counsel?

Day 5   In what way do I offer guidance or counsel to others?

Day 6   The ways I have witnessed priests acting for justice are…

Day 7   How do I stand up for justice in the world?

Week Thirty
Focus: *Advent, a time of Waiting and Preparing*

Day 1   Why is waiting important in my life?

Day 2   In what way do I need to prepare my heart and mind for this Advent?

Day 3   How have I balanced waiting and preparing for Christ with Christmas preparation?

Day 4   In what way do I celebrate the season of Advent in my home and with others?

Day 5   I offer hope to others by…

Day 6   What forms of darkness do I recognize in the world?

Day 7   What do I need for Christ's light to shine through me?

Week Thirty-one
Focus: *Christmas*

Day 1   Christmas gives me the feeling of…

Day 2   The Incarnation challenges me by…

Day 3   How am I challenged by Jesus as a baby?

Day 4   In what way has new birth taken place within my life?

Day 5   How have I perceived God's message coming to me?

Day 6   What gift of self-have I given?

Day 7   What in my heart do I lay at the manger?

Week Thirty-two
Focus: *Mary*

Day 1   Where I have recently followed Mary's example and replied, "Yes" to God?

Day 2   When in my life have I faced fear?

Day 3   When did I last feel joy overflowing inside of me? Why?

Day 4   What positive outcome has resulted from struggles in my life?

Day 5   In what way have I been pushed into situations before I felt ready?

Day 6   When have I had to let go of someone important to me?

Day 7   In what way have I suffered a broken heart out of love for God?

Week Thirty-three
Focus: *Morals and My Decision Making*

Day 1   In what way have my morals become stronger?

Day 2   How have my morals affected my decisions since initiation?

Day 3   My relationships reflect my morals by…

Day 4   My morals are challenged by…

Day 5   In what way has belonging to a church community given me support and encouragement in living out my morals?

Day 6   How does the Eucharist give me strength to live morally?

Day 7   How has my prayer life affected my moral decision-making?

Week Thirty-four
Focus: *Our Call to Discipleship*

Day 1   In what way have I deepened my understanding of discipleship?

Day 2   I have responded to Christ's call to be his disciple by…

Day 3   How does being Christ's disciple challenge my attitude towards love?

Day 4   In what way has my practice of forgiveness grown?

Day 5   How do others see Christ reflected in my actions?

Day 6   Who are the disciples I travel with in life?

Day 7   How much do I need community? Why?

Week Thirty-five

Focus: *Rites – Sending to Election and Call to Continuing Conversion*

Day 1   Knowing that the church keeps record of my name I feel…

Day 2   In what way have I fully embraced the gospel way of life?

Day 3   What growth has there been in my capacity to give and receive love?

Day 4   How have I contributed to the growth of my church community?

Day 5   In what way do I share my freedom in Christ with others?

Day 6   In what way do I see myself as a child of God?

Day 7   What stirrings of conversion do I continue to have?

Week Thirty-six
Focus: *Purification and Enlightenment*

Day 1   In what way do I no longer fear to recognize temptation in my life?

Day 2   The greatest transformation in my life is….

Day 3   In what way do I share my thirst for Christ with others?

Day 4   What do I now see that I chose to ignore before?

Day 5   In what way do I step out of myself to be involved in community life?

Day 6   Christ continues to enter my life through….

Day 7   The Passion of Christ challenges me by…

Week Thirty-seven
Focus: *Saints in our lives*

Day 1   What particular saint has affected my faith journey in an important way? Why?

Day 2   What characteristics of this saint am I challenged by?

Day 3   What similarities do I share with this saint?

Day 4   In what way has my faith grown stronger by having a saint as a role model?

Day 5   When I think of myself as being holy…..

Day 6   How does my worshiping community reflect the communion of saints?

Day 7   In what way does my life reflect holiness to the world?

Week Thirty-eight
Focus: *Prayers of our Church – The Creed and Our Father*

Day 1   When I stand with my community to share in the Creed I feel…

Day 2   The portion of the Creed that resonates in my heart and mind is…

Day 3   In what way do I live out the four marks of the church, "one, holy, catholic and apostolic"?

Day 4   In what way do I feel connected to all of life when I say, "Our Father"?

Day 5   How do I see heaven and earth being related through the Lord's Prayer?

Day 6   What have I come to depend upon as my "daily bread"?

Day 7   How easily do I extend forgiveness to others?

Week Thirty-nine
Focus: *Holy Week – Overview*

Day 1   What are my feelings and thoughts as I enter Holy Week?

Day 2   In what way do I experience a movement closer to Christ?

Day 3   What change is required of me?

Day 4   In what way do I still hide from the light?

Day 5   As one praying in the "garden" with Christ I feel…

Day 6   I stand at the cross because…

Day 7   In what way do I find quiet and silence challenging?

Week Forty
Focus: *Holy Thursday*

Day 1   As the holy oils are presented to my parish community I feel…

Day 2   In what way have I allowed the oil of the sick, the oil of catechumen or the holy chrism to permeate my faith journey?

Day 3   Do I hesitate having my feet washed like Peter? Why or why not?

Day 4   The washing of feet calls me to…

Day 5   What do I recall as bread is broken and wine is poured?

Day 6   In what way do I stay in prayer, keep vigil, with Christ?

Day 7   How do I respond when recognized as a follower of Christ?

Week Forty-one
Focus: *Good Friday*

Day 1   As I experience Good Friday I feel…

Day 2   What passages or verses of the bible do I reflect on? Why?

Day 3   How necessary is silence or quiet for my experience of this day?

Day 4   What do I imagine as taking place in the tomb of Jesus?

Day 5   How have I experienced conversion of heart?

Day 6   In what way do I venerate the cross in my daily life?

Day 7   When I touch the cross I feel…

Week Forty-two
Focus: *Holy Saturday*

Day 1   My preparation for celebrating Easter involves…

Day 2   In what way have I received guidance in my preparation for Easter?

Day 3   What teaching has offered me encouragement for faith growth?

Day 4   What gives me courage to face the unknown?

Day 5   How am I ready to take risks for my faith in Christ?

Day 6   The freedom I have experienced in Christ is…

Day 7   In what way do I feel challenged to reveal Christ's love to others?

Week Forty-three
Focus: *Easter Vigil - Fire and Light*

Day 1   In what way did the fire of the Holy Spirit illuminate my love of God?

Day 2   "Christ yesterday and today, the beginning and the end, Alpha, and Omega, all time belongs to him, and all the ages, to him be glory and power, through every age forever. By his holy and glorious wounds may Christ our Lord guard us and keep us." These words challenge me today because…

Day 3   What is Christ's light helping me see today?

Day 4   What responsibility does a lighted processional candle call me to?

Day 5   Where is Christ's light leading me now?

Day 6   How does my life proclaim Christ's light today?

Day 7   As I remember my initiation, Christ calls me to…

Week Forty-four
Focus: *Easter Vigil - Salvation*

Day 1   Salvation through Christ's Paschal Mystery offers me….

Day 2   Salvation, freely given, causes me to feel…

Day 3   How do I sacrifice myself in everyday life?

Day 4   What demonstration of love in my life reflects Christ's love for me?

Day 5   In what way do I feel immersed in Christ's love?

Day 6   Who are those in my life who love unselfishly?

Day 7   What unselfish action will I give today?

Week Forty-five
Focus: *Easter Vigil – Paschal Mystery of Jesus Christ*

Day 1   The importance of Jesus' birth for me is…

Day 2   A favorite teaching of Jesus that guides my life is… Why?

Day 3   What story told by Jesus best reflects my relationships?

Day 4   In what way does the fact that Jesus lived challenge society today?

Day 5   What impact does Jesus' death and resurrection have upon my view of life?

Day 6   How do I spread the good news of Jesus?

Day 7   What are the ways I help to build the kingdom of God?

Week Forty-six
Focus: *Easter Vigil - Water of life*

Day 1   What meaning does water hold for me in life?

Day 2   My favorite body of water is…. because….

Day 3   Water feeds my spirit by…

Day 4   When I am blessed with holy water I feel…

Day 5   When I remember my baptismal waters I am challenged by….

Day 6   In what way does my baptism free me to see truth?

Day 7   What actions do I continue to take to live the life of Christ?

Week Forty-seven

Focus: *Easter Vigil - My Baptismal Candle*

Day 1   In what way has the light of Christ shown through my darkness?

Day 2   How does the light of Christ help me to see more clearly?

Day 3   What responsibility do I have to the light of Christ?

Day 4   In what way do I pass on the light of Christ?

Day 5   How does my community share in lighting the way for others with Christ's light?

Day 6   How is the church challenged in carrying the light of Christ?

Day 7   In what way does the light of Christ connect humanity?

Week Forty-eight
Focus: *Easter Vigil - My White garment*

Day 1   The white garment I wore at my baptism was…

Day 2   Putting on the white garment symbolizing purification caused me to feel…

Day 3   In what way do I still see myself as "putting on Christ"?

Day 4   The meaning of the white garment calls me to see myself as….

Day 5   The meaning of the white garment calls me to see others as…

Day 6   In what way do I offer an example of "wearing" Christ?

Day 7   What challenges me when I "wear" Christ outside my church community?

Week Forty-nine
Focus: *Intercessions – Prayers of the Faithful*

Day 1   How does my baptism relate to my participation in the prayers of the faithful?

Day 2   When I hear the community in prayer I feel…because…

Day 3   In what way do I feel connected by listening and responding during the intercessions?

Day 4   What can be gained by praying for the needs of the church?

Day 5   What affect does prayer have upon the world?

Day 6   In what way is the community brought together as one when praying for those in need?

Day 7   How do the prayers of the faithful affect those of my household?

Week Fifty
Focus: *Bread and Wine – food for the journey*

Day 1   How "hungry" for Christ do I feel? Why?

Day 2   In what way do I see myself as the bread and wine in the presentation of the gifts?

Day 3   When I participate in the sacrifice at the altar I see…

Day 4   In what way do I see my life being broken for others?

Day 5   How is my life poured out for others?

Day 6   The body and blood of Christ challenge me to become…

Day 7   I need the body and blood of Christ because….

Week Fifty-one
Focus: *Mystagogia – breaking open the mysteries*

Day 1   I tasted…

Day 2   I heard…

Day 3   I felt…

Day 4   I saw…

Day 5   My heart and mind were touched by…

Day 6   I will never forget…

Day 7   I am still challenged by…

Week Fifty-two
Focus: *Called to Serve*

Day 1   How do I feel about serving others?

Day 2   What skills and talents do I have to share with others?

Day 3   What actions have I seen within the community that offer me example of service?

Day 4   How is prayer helping me to hear the call to serve?

Day 5   Who are those people I trust to help me in determining my call to service?

Day 6   What encouragement and support do I have from family members?

Day 7   I feel called to serve because....

www.ingramcontent.com/pod-product-compliance
Lightning Source LLC
Chambersburg PA
CBHW050733010526
44107CB00010B/836